The Copenhagen Deception

By Platinum F Morgan

Cobalt Dog Press, LLC

The Copenhagen Deception

A Cobalt Press Book

All Rights reserved

Copyright © 2022 Platinum F Morgan

First Edition

ISBN: 978-1-953844-01-9

*Dedicated to
the workers,
the inventors,
engineers,
and the true scientists,
who seek a better world.*

"I am confident that here truly is such a thing as living again, that the living spring from the dead, and that the souls of the dead are in existence." —
Socrates

Contents

Introduction..7
About the Author...9
Failure of the "Law of Attraction"..11

Part I Dreaming of the Future

September 11, 2001...19
John W Dunne..25
Bitcoin & my Twilight Zone Experience.....................................29
The Mandela Effect...39
The Dress..45
The Fall of 2016 Everything Will Change..................................49
The Sports Almanac..55
The Rapture...61

Part II The Science

The Double Slit Experiment..71
The Copenhagen Deception..77
Schrodinger's Cat..81
The Theory of the Universal Wave Function..............................85
The Event..91

Part III Demonic Infiltration Strategy

The Adversary...101
The Time Travelers...105
Mistakes of the Founders of the USA.......................................109
Psychological Warfare..111
The Difference between Freedom and Slavery.........................117
Tribal...125
Infiltration of the Tribe..127
The Mistake of assuming common ground with Evil............... 131
Unknowns...137
The Failsafe...141
Afterword..147

Introduction

In this book I will attempt to put into words certain concepts about the nature of reality.

While doing this I shall describe good and evil. For example I may describe a certain person or social economic group of having a negative intention or positive intention toward others or of the world in general.

Many people reading this have knowledge about the fundamental forces of the Universe:

Gravity

Electromagnetism

Strong Nuclear Force

Weak Nuclear Force

I have a hypothesis that what people know as "good" and "evil" are real energetic forces , these are just as real as the known fundamental forces mention above.

I am mentioning this now for a reason. This "evil" or "negative" force appears to have an effect on the brains in most people's heads to various degrees of influence.

This is the beginning of deception.

This evil force has the effect of appearing as one's own thoughts. In the following chapters, I will cover concepts that this evil force or whatever is directing this evil force, does not want you to investigate further.

Some of you, who have made it this far will continue reading this book, motivated by curiosity.
Then at some point you will suddenly get offended with something or some concept, that is being convened. The desire to reject the concept will be so strong that you will believe that it is your idea to stop reading this book, and think something like "this is delusional, or conspiracy theory".
These are commands from agents of "the devil's matrix".

Their greatest power is convincing you that, their thoughts are your thoughts..

They have many tools of deception. One is to use the desire of a people to do good against them.

When I am describing the malice of a person or group, I am not attacking that person or group. I am criticizing that negative actions or intentions that particular individual or group is manifesting. My point is that they are a captured mind that is being deceived into manifesting this evil, because the evil force has convinced them that they are doing it for their own benefit. They allowed their minds to become batteries in the devil's matrix.

You the reader may have empathy for the person or group I am criticizing and start to think negatively of me the author. Your empathy is real and it is honorable, but this evil is so great at deception that it will twist and use you own empathy, positive intentions against you. They do this in order to deceive you into supporting and defending the evil intention that is directing them.

About the Author

A little about my background.

Do to the nature of the information I am going to disclose, I am using a pen name and will be minimizing the disclosure personal details, however I know that there is a need to include some basic information about my life to dispel certain assumptions that will be spouted by the critics of this book should it ever reach a large enough readership.

As I write this I am currently in my 40's getting paid an hourly wage to work in manufacturing. I do this by choice, however I am not sitting in my garage next to a Lamborghini. In the past I have also held positions of rank. I have been invited to meetings in large cities and dined with multi million dollar corporate executives on a few occasions. I have also been to a number of private small "parties" with people who's net worth are in the 7 figures. In fact when the great recession hit during the fall of 2008, I started making plans to start a business on the side while I still held a decent position in a company, because I saw the signs that the ax was going to begin swinging and I knew it was only a matter of time before it would swing in my direction.

About the time this was happening there was a big buzz in the media about this Law of Attraction and an interesting movie called "The Secret".

When the day came that I was sitting in a conference room being handed a severance package, I was totally high on blind optimism. I knew now that I can devote myself full time to the business I started, I was going to succeed. It hadn't made a profit during the

2 years I was working on it part time while I also worked the full time job, in fact I was feeding it money to burn during those 2 years. I took my severance and added the company stock (I sold) to it and put it all in my business and went all in.

Three years later……

Then one day after spending about a year working a few weeks or months at back breaking low pay jobs separated by weeks at a time of making zero money, I found myself driving to a job interview for a decent paying job, not a position of rank, but one of the better working class blue color jobs around. I was taking the last of my coins and pennies to get cash to put gas in my car.

What went wrong?

I spent years during and after my spectacular failure, gathering information in an attempt to solve that question. I believe in cause and effect. I also believe when solving a problem, that when you eliminate the impossible, what ever remains no matter how crazy or delusional it appears, must be the solution.

Failure of the "Law of Attraction"

Why did the "Law of Attraction" fail for me?

What is the real secret?

What was I attempting to accomplish?

I guess the real question to ask is what did I want to get rich for?

What plans did I have for the money?

After spending years searching for the answer as to why "the Law of Attraction" failed, I realized the main thing I was looking for was a better world, Justice, Respect. I would add Meritocracy, however that falls under the umbrella of Justice.

Consider the following:

What is the world you would prefer?

What are you working towards?

Now in my own life my plan was to use the surplus wealth I created toward solving the problems I witnessed in this world. Raising the standard of living of the people, expanding freedom, and Justice.

Now imagine a world that has no massive police states, or government tyrannies on Earth. No war or violent crime. The average working man lived an upper middle class lifestyle while only working about 20 hours a week on average

Almost everyone had strong, healthy lifetimes averaging 400 to 500 years.

If you lived in such a world and you noticed a tiny faction of the population (perhaps 0.5 to 1 %) starting to advocate for regular wars, shorter lifespans for most of the population, and most of the ownership of property being transferred to themselves, while arguing for the construction of a coercive police state to carry out the corruption of that world, would you be offended?

The real secret is that this is their world, this is the world they corrupted. The Secret (Law of Attraction) was failing for most people because we were basing our world view on a false premise.

That false premise being that they wanted the same thing as me. But those were not problems to be solved. They prefer the world the way it is. They crave a world of masters and slaves, and they intend to be the masters.

The evidence in my experience is that, most of the "Rich and successful" don't have positive intentions towards the rest of humanity. Their intentions are negative. (With the few exceptions proving the rule, i. e. how almost all the billionaires of the world united in opposition to Donald J Trump, after he began to stand for the blue collar working man) Once I saw how obvious this is, the other pieces of the puzzle began to fall into place.

After studying the rulers of this world for years, it is time for me to expose the cheat code that has allowed them to corrupt this world.

Now let me explain what I mean by cheat code. Gamers who have played multiplayer online games with competitive leader boards will understand my explanation. I use to be somewhat more than casual with competitive online gaming. Sometimes there would be a player or even small group of players who would suddenly start crushing everyone else. When it happened to me I would be puzzled as to how someone would seem to be magically unbeatable. Then later it would be discovered that they were using some sort of exploit or cheat code that the rest of us did not know about..

Now the thing about such exploits or cheat codes is that they are only effective to the extent no one else knows about the cheat code. Once the other players learn the exploit or cheat code, the competitive advantage it bestowed on the few is wiped out. In video games, there was mainly two ways the devs would deal with the cheat code once they discovered it.

1. They would patch the exploit.

Or

2. Allow all players to use the cheat code.

In either of these cases the unfair competitive advantage to the few who kept it from the rest was removed.

It was around late 2013 to middle of 2014 that I realized exactly what this cheat code is. This realization took place when I had the twilight zone experience.

Many readers, might be asking, what is the twilight zone experience?

Years ago there was an episode of The Twilight Zone that first aired on March 21, 1986.
It is titled:

"Need to Know"

It starts out with a man whispering into another mans ear, the true secret of existence. However, the truth is so mind blowing that anyone who hears it, goes insane. I believe I had this experience (or something similar) in the winter, late 2013 to early 2014. I'm not claiming to be insane, however, I have considered to possibility that I may be insane.
It was during this experience, that many pieces of the puzzle suddenly came together, to form a coherent picture or blueprint of this cheat code. It was then I realized what happened to this world.

Around that time I began research for evidence supporting my conclusions about this cheat code, and to see if others knew or were talking about it. Throughout those years sometimes months would go by were all my spare time was spent researching this cheat code. Countless hours watching and archiving youtube videos, analyzing social media for evidence that others are seeing this.
Then in the fall of 2015 before the first presidential primary were even held some information was showing up in my research and analysis showing Donald Trump winning not only the Republican nomination but also winning the general election a year later in the fall of 2016, along with other things, sports games, etc coming true in that same time period.

I will get into that, later in this book.

I want to first start with the events of September 11, 2001.

Part I

Dreaming of the Future

September 11, 2001

As far back as I can remember, I was never a morning person. I guess getting woken up as a child to go to school turned me off to mornings. Hence, I made it a point in my adult life, to always apply or bid on jobs that are evening or night shift (also known as 2nd or 3rd shift). In 2001 I was in my mid 20's and renting a 3rd floor "bachelor pad" in a small town. Since at the time I had arranged my affairs to have a 2nd shift blue color job, I had a routine of waking up earlier some days to do laundry and pick up some burgers at the local restaurant about 2 blocks walking distance down the street.

My mornings would always begin with me turning the radio on to listen to music while I got ready. That morning I woke up about 10:15 am Eastern time, as I was in the Eastern time zone. I could not find any music on the radio, and I kept changing stations in frustration. I distinctly remember hearing talk of a new plane crash in western Pennsylvania. It boggled my mind why a plane crash would cause all the stations to be talking news and not playing music. I turned my radio off and finished gathering my clothes to drop off at the laundry mat before I go to the local diner get a burger.

I walked into the diner to order my usual burger and fries and see people staring a a TV in the corner. I hear someone say "look, there it goes!" Then I turn to look at the screen to see a video of one of the twin towers in New York being destroyed in a controlled demolition.

Later watching the news reports and reading the papers, it was being reported that the towers collapse from the heat of the jet fuel. This had to be a lie. That was clearly a controlled demolition, especially later when I found out another building came down in a controlled demolition and was not hit by a plane. This was the first major public display, I've seen that there is an incredible deception happening in the world.

Why would such a deception be taking place?

Why lie to cover up a controlled demolition, and why do such a thing while people are in the building?

While justice demands answers to those questions, there is something much more profound about September 11, 2001. It is the first time, I can find in my research, a preponderance of evidence exists that information can be sent backwards in a timeline, and/or there is more than one timeline. What I mean by this is that, in my research, it appears that large events seem to send a shockwave backwards as well as forward in time. Or at least it appears that way. Some have called this "retro-causality" others refer to it as "reverse determination".

I remember hearing reports of many "lucky coincidences", where people who were going to be at ground zero were prevented from being there by circumstances of the days, hours, or minutes leading up to the event. A young lady was planning to meet two of her friends at one of the towers. Her mother convinced her not to go on September 11, and she survived (sadly losing her other two friends who still went.) A man's car had a sudden breakdown on the way to his job at the towers. Then there are numerous unsubstantiated stories of people who, choose to call off work because they had a gut feeling.

I read some conflicting reports of random number generators around the planet suddenly spiking minutes or hours before the event, however, I could not substantiate those reports one way or the other.

The most striking evidence, is the album covers.

There is documented evidence of three separate bands putting out albums that year with album covers eerily resembling events of September 11, 2001. In fact one of the album's original confirmed release date was September 11, 2001

A rap group called "Inner City Hustlers", from Houston, Texas, released an album called "Time to Explode around the time of July 2001. This album cover had twin towers with some resemblance to the World Trade Center in New York City. I discovered in my research that the designer of that album cover was questioned by the FBI after the towers were destroyed on September 11, 2001.

Another rap group from Oakland, California, called "The Coup" had planned to release an album called "Party Music" in September 2001. The original cover of "Party Music" appears almost identical to some of the most recognizable videos and still photos of the second plan hitting the towers on September 11, 2001, in spite of the fact that that album cover was designed at least months before the event, it depicts.

Then there was a metal group called "Dream Theater" from Boston, Massachusetts. Their album was called "Live Scenes from New York". The image on the cover of the CD had an apple wrapped in twine, on top of the apple is a burning Manhattan skyline, including the World Trade Center. The original release date was September 11, 2001.

Band leader (at the time) Mike Portnoy announced on the band's website - *"I can only say that it is a horrible coincidence that we obviously could have never forseen. The timing of the release of the CD happening on the very same day as this tragedy is merely an incredible coincidence."*

At this point, I will point out that album release dates are planned weeks to months in advance, to allow for planned blitz promotion and coordinated marketing.

How is this possible?

I believe that people observing the events on September 11, 2001 were able to somehow send the information back to their past selves. It appears based on my research that the information received, then was implanted into the subconscious of those people to create those album cover designs in the past. Some people may have witnessed their own death or the death of someone else, and they had a gut feeling, thereby allowing them to avoid it in their future.

John W Dunne

*"Row, row, row your boat,
Gently down the stream.
Merrily, merrily, merrily, merrily,
Life is but a dream."*

Did you ever have a dream where you were living your life and not know it was a dream until you woke up?

Did you ever have a dream, then years later experience events happen just like it happened in the dream or similar?

In 1927 a man named John William Dunne, published a book called An Experiment with Time.

The book was inspired by Mr Dunne's own precognitive dreams of his own future. Mr Dunne, seems to put forth the argument that the moment "now" (AKA the present) is not described by science. He called his theory "Serialism". In it he appears to make the case that time itself exists in more than one dimension. There is a base world or perfect world where no "mistakes" exist. In that world there is no such thing as death and we exist as eternal immortal beings. The worlds outside of it are less perfect as one travels away from it. However, the consciousness that exists in this imperfect world will snap back to another world across the time dimensions when we make mistakes in the less than perfect worlds.

I believe this is how the people were able to witness the events of September 11, 2001, before it happened. Somehow it wasn't just the information that got sent back, but a portion of their consciousness snapped back, along a time dimension. Perhaps to a parallel universe similar to the one they died in.

I've had experiences where I dreamed of the future. They are usually only mundane everyday life situations.
I also had a few dreams where it was almost like a warning, that I was on the wrong path. In one such dream I was in prison wearing an orange jumpsuit. I ignored the warning and within 24 hours was arrested and wearing an orange jumpsuit in real life. While this was many years ago when I was young and naive, the point is that, I was given the warning and failed to avoid the situation.

While researching the cheat code, I would look back at the costly mistakes I made in my life, and while I do regret my mistakes, I did them out of naivety, not willful malice. I point this out because when I realized what the cheat code represented, I saw how there are people in this world whose intentions are malice. They seem to know and take advantage of the naivety of the rest of the population. These are the true rulers of this world. The highest among them operate like Biff with his sports almanac from the future. Using their knowledge of future events to push the rest of us around.

I did not know this until 2014 after having my twilight zone experience.

Bitcoin & my Twilight Zone Experience

"I think of going to the grave without having a psychedelic experience like going to the grave without ever having sex. It means that you never figured out what it is all about." - Terence McKenna

"The problem is not to find the answer, it's to face the answer." - Terence McKenna

In 2012 I invested a small amount of money into Bitcoin. I thought it was interesting, but didn't expect it to become as big as it eventually did. If I had any idea I would have bought more.

The thing that really distracted me from paying as much attention to Bitcoin as I should have, was the 2012 phenomenon.

There was a mass amount of hype about how something was going to happen in December of 2012. There were many theories being talked about at the time. One of the main ones having to do with the end of the Mayan calendar. Some were talking about the world could end, some were saying that there was going to be a dimensional shift, and collision of universes, nuclear war, even alien invasion.

The one that fascinated me the most was Terence McKenna's time-wave theory. He claimed that there was some inevitable event in the future, where time was going to change somehow. He claimed he didn't know exactly when it was going to happen, but said there was a good possibility that the end of the Mayan calendar could line up with this event. He also said it may not happen on that day, and could still be years in our subjective futures.

Then when 2012 ended with a whimper, I considered the possibility that McKenna's time-wave event is still in the future. However, the events of 2013 up until my twilight zone experience in the beginning of 2014, cause me to consider the possibility that this event is inevitable but I don't know how far in the future it is.

During 2013, I spent my spare time researching Bitcoin. As it went up in value I lurked on a few websites that discussed Bitcoin, sites like bitcointalk and a subreddit called r/Bitcoin. That was when I began to notice something intriguing.

As Bitcoin was rising into the hundreds of dollars per Bitcoin, there were new people commenting in those forums. These people were not there to have an intelligent discussion. There was an underlying hostility in the tone of their comments. At first I did not know the reason for the hostility.

You see, I spent most of my life as a blue collar working class man. As such, I could not understand why people would suddenly be angry that Bitcoin was going up in real value, setting records along the way. I spent time researching some of these people who were angry about the success of Bitcoin. My first false assumption was that these were other working class people who were envious because they missed the boat, and were there to vent.

Most of us blue collar working class folks are taught that we are the ones envious of the managerial class. Whenever we speak about being treated unfairly they respond that we are just being envious of the "success" of the managerial class. Most blue collar working class people believe in things like meritocracy, and fairness. We tend to project our own virtues onto others like the managerial class. That is to say, we assume that they "earned it".

However, my research was showing that these people who were angry about the success of Bitcoin were mainly white collar managerial, and had some degree of independent wealth. This made no sense to me.

Why were people of independent wealth, angry that some blue collar folks may become financially independent?

Toward the end of 2013 when Bitcoin was approaching 1,000 dollars per coin, I started getting invited to some private "social events" with other people of wealth. I notice that once one is known to get some degree of wealth, they start getting invited to the "club". Now this doesn't necessarily mean you are in the club. In reality they are testing out a potential new member. Some of the club were interested in Bitcoin, but only as another tool they can use to their own advantage. But there were some who would speak against Bitcoin with a condescending hostility. I would patiently attempt to correct them. I was still projecting my own kindness onto these people. I thought they were bashing Bitcoin out of ignorance. Later I found out that some of the very people who were trash talking Bitcoin, were also invested in it at the same time. They were attempting to deceive me into doubting myself. But it was worse than that. Those were the outright forked tongue deceivers.

The more honest among them would openly brag about treating the blue collar working class unfairly.

I remember sometimes over the years conversations among blue collar people about being treated unfairly by management. The few occasions (usually at meetings) when an hourly worker spoke up about being treated unfairly, the manager would always act all righteous, and flip it around and imply the worker is just lazy and/or stupid.

Now, what I learned at my private meetings with the club is worse. As bad as the blue collar may perceive the managerial class hostility. I have had private conversations where they confess their absolute contempt for the working class. These people are almost without exception total scumbags. In fact many of them are outright satanists or luciferians, but I digress.

Another thing I noticed on those forums like r/Bitcoin were people talking about how cool it would be to go back in time and invest in Bitcoin before it skyrocketed in value. I found this idea interesting mainly because the same thought already crossed my mind. Now, I have invested in other things like conventional stocks and precious metals before. None of those things would make me rich on a scale if I had one shot to go back a few years and invest in them. To be sure I'd have more money, but not independently wealthy the way I could be if I invested early in Bitcoin. This was because most of the money made on those stocks were made by the club, before they were even listed on a stock exchange (i. e. before the IPO). Bitcoin was unique in modern history as something that the everyday blue collar worker could invest in at an early stage. It was then, in that thought experiment, that I began to realize why the managerial class was pissed about the success of Bitcoin.

The managerial class weren't just mad about some blue collar people getting some wealth. **You see, the very existence of Bitcoin, (and its success) was starting to reveal the exploit, the cheat code.**

The Twilight Zone Experience

On a few rare times in my life I have been able to procure various mind altering substances. While most of my psychedelic

experiences involved smoking cannabis, I was able by pure circumstance to get my hands on something more powerful. The first time I cautiously took a small amount, just enough to barely feel the effects.
The second time I took what my research said is a standard trip size dose. I sat in my office and listened to music as the effect hit me.

Words cannot do justice to what happened next. Somehow my mind expanded to a state that can barely be comprehended outside of that state. It was like that scene in the movie The Matrix where Morpheus says, "Unfortunately, no one can be told what the Matrix is. You have to see it for yourself."

While I was in that state, I was able to understand the true meaning of existence. It was in that state, the cheat code was fully revealed to me. I saw how it was all connected. I understood that death is some type of illusion. This world where most of the population was poor, was a totally fraud. The idea that the working class people were poor because they didn't work hard enough, or that they were lazy was a huge deception.
It was there that I saw how the true rulers of this world, what some call the Deep State or Cabal, (what I call the Power Monopoly) were being guided by demonic forces. These demonic beings or demons seem to feed off of negative emotions. They are truly sadistic.
Most of the billionaires of this world were guided into that position by those demonic beings. There appears to be some sort of agreement or contract between the human and the demonic being. They (the human servant) must use that wealth for evil. It is as if they are a group of Biffs with sports almanacs, using their temporal advantage to buy controlling interests in all critical infrastructure as well as media. They understood by their limited knowledge of the future given to them, that they would need to control media and communications. It is these people who

occupy all most all positions of rank within all the governments of this world.

It is in learning how they got their feet on the neck of the world that, I saw the solution to the problem.

While I was in that experience, I saw that the stories of the Bible, specifically, rapture, resurrection and eternal life were, without a doubt, true. I understood that this has something to do with what some people refer to as parallel universes, and others called the many worlds theory.

What is Sin?

What is the narrow path?

How does one pass through the eye of the needle?

What is the eye of the needle?

All of these questions were answered.

I also saw how Terence McKenna's time-wave theory was connected to all of it.

Some of what I learned is personal. Some can't be put into words. However, I learned some other things.

What people refer to as the rapture is an inevitable event along a timeline, that seems to cut across the parallel universes at some sort of angle.

Try to imagine the distant past and the far future somehow folding together like a book and smashing everything in between until everyone who ever lived was alive at the same time. This appears to be the event that Terence McKenna was describing.

These parallel universes are the solution to the problem of freewill.

This brings us back to the cheat code and the demonic problem. It became clear while researching this book that the main strategy of the Power Monopoly is deceiving the people that they are ruling over, into believing this is the only world. At first it did not make sense to me. If there are unlimited parallel universes, why would they care if people believe in them or not?

The answer is simple, in the paradise world I am working toward, it would not matter if people believed in the existence of lesser worlds, because positive emotion is not dependent on deception. However, the existence of negative emotions in this twisted world is dependent on the slaves believing that there is no real escape.

Is it now becoming clear what is going on here?

Or am I a few fries short of a happy meal?

Truth be told, I have considered that possibility.

Perhaps I am really wearing a straitjacket, drooling in a mental institution?

While I was researching this book, I discovered a wise man said, it is basically pointless to worry about going insane, because if you really are going insane, there is nothing you can do about it anyhow.

I came to the conclusion that there are two main ways to break the Power Monopoly and free the slaves of this world. One is to show people that this power must be eventuality available to them, if they can learn the true nature of reality. The other is the exposure of the cheat code and showing the evidence that they have embarked on a strategy of concealing this temporal advantage, to those who would use this power to be free.

I saw how this two pronged strategy can be used as a pincer movement, across parallel universes and timelines to defeat them. Also I saw this years before the movie by Mr Nolan. Although I have no way of proving it, yet.

Also Mr Nolan's movie is centered on the premise of one world determinism, while I am arguing for many worlds determinism. Hence the war is much more complicated in a way, but simpler in others.

Up until this point everything can be dismissed as a psychedelic trip. Hence, I spent the last few years researching to find scientific evidence that what I learned is true.

The Mandela Effect

"It's a beautiful day in this neighborhood" - Mister Rogers

While I've heard of the Mandela Effect, I didn't spend much time investigating it until after my twilight zone experience.

It is named after a man named Nelson Mandela, who later became the President of South Africa.

Apparently there are people who remember him dying in prison years before he was released and became President. This became used as a general name to describe the effect of having memories of an alternate history of the world. I was fascinated with this because, this is one of the key pieces of evidence that this is not the only world.

When I say evidence, I mean objective witness based evidence. For example it only takes two witnesses to testify to an event to put someone away for serious crimes like high treason. While here there are hundreds if not, thousands who seem to have these alternative memories of history.

There are numerous examples that people have written about. Such as:

There is an alternative world where The Berenstain Bears are spelled differently. Some people at first thought the name was only changed on the internet. They dug some of their old books out of their attic and were shocked to see the new spelling on those old books.

Disagreeing about certain lines in old movies like Star wars, when Dark Vader says he is Luke's father.

Or the movie Field of dreams. "If you build it, they will come"

While I found most of theses things mildly interesting, I didn't really have conflicting memories about the above mentioned examples. I have no memories of Nelson Mandela dying in prison. I really can't say I had alternative memories of The Berenstain Bears. In fact my memory of Star Was matched the line in the movie where Vader said, "No, I am your father".

But the Field of Dreams is when I began to doubt myself. However, that was not enough.

The things that really hit me are Mister Roger's Neighborhood, and the original Disney movie Snow White.

The song at the beginning of Mister Roger's Neighborhood, he is singing, "It's a beautiful day in this neighborhood," while I have memories of a world where he is singing:
"It's a beautiful day in the neighborhood."

In Snow White, the evil queen speaks to the mirror and says, "magic mirror on the wall, who is the fairest one of all," while I have memories of a world where the evil queen says:
"Mirror mirror, on the wall, who is the fairest one of all"

I remember a dash on Kit – Kat bars.

What I found most intriguing while investigating the Mandela Effect, was the emergence of evidence that other people were beginning to witness the dark forces, (i. e. demonic influence) among the population in real time. Some of them refer to this as "The Download". Some call it "going Smith" like the agent in the Matrix movies.

Basically, there will be a conversation where a person is presented with evidence, that this is not the only world, like for example evidence of the Mandela Effect. The person will usually at first look at the evidence and agree that there is something to it. That is to say, they will seem to remember some things changing or having different memories. Then, like the matrix movies, the expression on their face will change like an agent of the matrix is being downloaded into them. At this point, it is like the original person is no longer there. There is some demonic influence, or possession, controlling the person. They will deny all the evidence, that other worlds exist.

I have witnessed this demonic influence on others. When trying to reason with them, I can sense that demonic entity's enjoyment, at taunting me. At that point I am no longer having an intelligent conversation with another human being. I am being taunted by a puppet controlled by a demonic entity.

I only include this information, because **the very act of the demons interfering to stop people from realizing that this is not the only world, is itself evidence, that this is not the only world.**

They are desperate to stop people from realizing this truth.

While people having disagreements about the past is interesting. What about people disagreeing about something in the present?

Is it possible for people to experience conflicting realities, in real time?

While I was having my experience I perceived many things. I also knew that there would come a time in the future before the end or rapture (although it is not really and end, but a new beginning) there would be times when people are experience conflicting realities in real time.
Not just disagreements about past memories.

The first such thing happened about a year after my experience.

The Dress

"Guys please help me - is this dress white and gold, or blue and black? Me and my friends can't agree and we are freaking... out." - Caitlin McNeill, February 2015

In early 2015, I started hearing talk about The Dress.

At this time I had already spent months looking for evidence of parallel universes. It became a daily hobby for me. I would spend an hour or more a day searching to see if others had similar experiences to mine.

At the time I was still working a low paying working class job in a factory. I even resigned from my position to decompress for a few months.

I started getting information crossing my desk about people looking at a picture of a dress and disagreeing about the color of it in real time. This was amazing. Of course I always saw the picture of the dress as white and gold. However, there was a significant portion of the population that claimed they were looking at a picture of a black and blue dress.

This happened late February through March of 2015.

There was much discussion about this for a few months. Some talked about the structures of the brain being different between those who perceived the conflicting dress colors. There were even a few scientific studies. One study involved 1,400 respondents, found that 57% saw the dress as blue and black; 30%

saw it as white and gold; 11% saw it as blue and brown; and 10% could switch between any of the color combinations.

The common theme in those studies indicates a difference in brain structure is what separates the people into their different color perception groups.

Up to this point I've had a basic working hypothesis that the human brain is a pattern shaped by the unbroken chain of causality events from the distant past to the future. This deterministic view would point to freewill being an illusion. That is if one assumes that the brain is a simple 3D object. However, if the brain is a 4D object then it is possible for freewill to exist in the 3D world. This also has the added bonus making individual death an illusion.

The Fall of 2016 everything will change.

While I was researching the concepts of parallel universes I discovered this character called Bashar.
This character known as Bashar turned out to be some being channeled by a man named Darryl Anka.

First I want to make it clear that I am in no way endorsing what I call "UFOOLOGY".

UFO is an acronym that stands for Unidentified Flying Object, nothing more.

I do believe there is life on other planets. In fact the main premise of this book is that there is some type of alien intelligent beings that are influencing the Earth currently and have been for most of recorded history.
I referred to these beings previously as demonic beings. It stands to reason that if there are bad beings, then there are also good beings. It is my opinion that this Bashar is a positive one.

I will respectfully disagree with Bashar's optimistic view of the "Law of Attraction". However, I find his description of the multiverse seemed to match my twilight zone experience.

I remember in late 2014 or sometime in early 2015, watching Darryl Anka speak and suddenly his voice changed.
He got more serious than I ever heard him speak before. He said that in the fall of 2016 everything would change. He even

repeated that message a few times. I thought it was interesting, because I knew in my gut that something was going to happen. I didn't know what it was exactly.

Then in the summer of 2015 I heard talk about Donald J Trump running for President of the united States of America. At the time I had planned to vote for Dr Rand Paul for President in the Republican primary. In fact I was even anti-Trump for a time. However, by the time my state held its primary Dr Paul had already dropped out of the race. So in April of 2016 I voted for Donald J Trump in the primary. But I am getting ahead of myself in this story. Lets go back to the fall of 2015.

Earlier in this book I mentioned how the real rulers of this world were a bunch of Biffs from back to the future with a temporal advantage of having knowledge of future events. Well interesting thing about that movie was, Marty McFly got the idea when Cubs win the world series in the fall of 2015. Biff takes the sports almanac and gives it to his younger self.

The Cubs came close in the autum of 2015 but fell short, in this world. I had a gut feeling that they were going to win in 2016. But that wasn't the big thing that caught my attention in the fall of 2015.

There was a sub on Reddit that spoke about stuff that was unusual, to put it mildly. Back in 2015, because of censorship and memory holing they had an unofficial policy of archiving posts especially if they were controversial.
This one caught my eye because it appeared to be evidence that backed up my hypothesis about the multiverse and the brain being a 3 dimensional slice of a 4 dimensional object. Back when I had my experience in early 2014, I understood that travel between parallel universes (or worlds if you prefer) would be like waking up from a very real dream. That is to say, individual consciousness upon reaching a mortal dead end, would transfer

from that failing 3D brain to another 3D brain, connected in the 4th dimension.

I would take it further, and postulate that the reason everyone dreams is because of the very fundamental problem of resolving cause and effect with freewill. The only solution I found so far points to the existence of these entangled worlds across time dimensions. I saw that each of us are sending ourselves into the future to learn and avoid fatal or near fatal dead ends in this 4 dimensional maze called life.

Many recognize the evidence of this as things like Deje Vue and/or dreaming of the future. It is clear that some can bring back more information about the future than others. Some learn to do this while awake, they call this "remote viewing". Some do this by training themselves to be able to remember their dreams.

That thing that caught my attention was the post around October 2015, on the internet site Reddit. As fate would have it, that entire post was archived shortly before it was deleted from Reddit. In this post someone claims to have dreamed of a future and then when the world turned into a nightmare, their consciousness snapped back to the past (i.e. they wake up in their subjective past). After reading that post and witnessing events play out the following months and years, it became clear to me that somehow this person was able to send their consciousness into a future world, then come back.

They described the election of 2016 with incredible detail, and even spoke about events to happen before and after the election. I even won a bet on the NFL playoffs based solely on this persons information they brought back. Interestingly there were details that diverged from the future world they witnessed. For example after winning that bet on one of the play off games I decided not to use the information to bet on the next game, because I had a gut feeling that things were going to start diverging. I turned out to be right as the final championships turned out different than he (or she?) predicted. Another example of a divergence, was the Vice Presidential candidates were different.

Watching events unfold over the years has only strengthened my resolve that my hypothesis is correct in some way. Unfortunately whoever wrote that, seems to have deleted their account on Reddit shortly after and disappeared before I could make contact, or attempt to.

Obviously that is just one example, but it is a strong one. I was actually getting many reports all during 2015 and 2016 of people dreaming that Donald J Trump would get elected President of the USA in the fall of 2016.

Why would all these people be dreaming about the election in the future?

Also, many of them did it back when his candidacy was considered a joke, and that Jeb Bush was going to win the republican nomination.

I believe that this is all connected to what Darryl Anka was referring to when he channeled the message about everything changing in the fall of 2016. Although he may or may not agree with me.

The Sports Almanac

"The pessimists went to America. The optimists went to Auschwitz." - Survivor of the holocaust

What is the Real Secret?

What is this exploit that has allowed a small group of people to enslave the world?

In the last chapter I mentioned that I disagree with the optimistic view of the "Law of Attraction". Now, I will qualify it.

The reason why things like "The Secret" and the "Law of Attraction" failed for most people is because it is based on a false premise. The deception being taught, is that if people ignore evil, then it will go away, or have no power.

They use different phrases for this deception:

"What you resist persists."

"Energy goes where attention flows."

The historical evidence has shown otherwise.

Things like "The Secret" and "Law of Attraction" became quite popular around the late 1800s and early 1900s. This idea of blind optimism. It was not until the NAZI Holocaust in the 1940s that this blind optimism, positive thinking trend was reversed. Hence the saying - "The pessimists went to America. The optimists went to Auschwitz."

Throughout most of my adult life, I've been a blue collar working class man. There were many stretches where I ended up going broke. There were times where I was living Just Over Broke (JOB) going paycheck to paycheck. If there was one thing that kept me there, it was my naivety. That is to say, my blind optimism.

Once I understood that there were real evil forces, working to keep me and others poor, I conducted my affairs accordingly. When I did this, my life changed. I was no longer broke. I also saw in hindsight how, conducting my affairs, with this strategy that there were evil people with malicious intentions, I would have avoided most of the problems, especially financial, in my life.

It was the experience I had, and the evidence I later discovered to corroborate it, that convinced me. From my twilight zone experience in early 2014 to reading about the people dreaming of the future, it was clear. This world is run by people who, through precognitive dreams, visions, among other things, have been able to seize a temporal advantage. They use this power and their positions they gained thereby to twist this world into a world of masters and slaves. They use their control of media, to push the optimism propaganda, so their prey will be pacified.

Henceforth I shall refer to people who have this temporal advantage (i. e. sports almanac holders) as Precogs.
There is a small percentage of the population that is using this power, and they are using it against the rest of us. However, they do need people to carry out their orders. These are the middle management, and government bureaucracy class. Henceforth I shall refer to them simply as the managerial class.

There are a number of ways that they recruit people to become a member of the management class. The most obvious way is by breeding, also know as putting their children into positions of rank. Of course since the Precogs, only represent a tiny portion of the population (for now) they need to recruit people willing to carry out evil, from among the greater portion of the populace.

I will not go into detail until the 2nd half of this book, about all the systems they use for control, at this time. However, I will give a fictionalized example of how they bring new recruits into middle management. In the following example the recruiter may of may not be a Precog. Going by the math, it is more likely that the recruiter is simply a member of the corrupt managerial class, and not an actual Precog.

Potential recruit : "What would it take for me to get ahead in life?"

Recruiter : "How would you like to earn 5 million dollars this years?"

Potential recruit : "I'd like that."

Recruiter : "You have to kill someone. Also you are guaranteed not to face criminal charges for it."

Potential recruit : "I'm not going to do that."

Recruiter : "Of course I'm not going to ask you to kill someone. How about for 2 million dollars you just break someone's legs ?"

Potential recruit : "I'm not going to break someone's legs."

Recruiter : "If you foreclose on some working class people's houses, we can pay you $250,000 plus bonus, for the number of foreclosures."

The above example is just one simplified and slightly exaggerated way recruits are corrupted by negotiating their soul away. The destination is the same. The man overseeing part of the control system to asset strip the working population of their property (the fruits of their labor) is no less a murderer. They are working for the advancement of the kingdom of Lucifer. Their final objective is simple, to kill, steal, and destroy.

The Rapture

When I was old enough to talk but still in the single digits in years, I was told about an event in the future. This was told to me by one of my grandparents. She spoke about how there would be a time where the people still alive at the time would not face death. I don't remember if she referred to it as the rapture, but would later realize that is would she was referring to. Now about 40 years after that conversation, I am writing this book. I've had over four decades to think about what this means.

In an earlier part of this book I write about the existence of parallel worlds. According to my lifetime of research, there are many of these worlds, some of them almost identical to this one, some worse, and some better. Apparently one of the best, if not the best world is referred to as heaven. I also believe there is a scale of paradise worlds between here and heaven. Going the other direction, the worlds get worse descending into hell.

This event was talked about for at least 2000 years.

In a previous chapter I wrote about the Precogs. Up until this point I was only speaking about the negative Precogs. Now I will begin an analysis of the good Precogs, starting with one of the most famous Precogs of all time, Jesus of the tribe of Judah.

In the Bible Jesus speaks about a time when there is a separation.

Matthew Chapter 24:

1. And Jesus went out, and departed from the temple: and his disciples came to *him* for to shew him the buildings of the temple.

2 And Jesus said unto them, See ye not all these things? verily I say unto you, There shall not be left here one stone upon another, that shall not be thrown down.

3 And as he sat upon the mount of Olives, the disciples came unto him privately, saying, Tell us, when shall these things be? and what *shall be* the sign of thy coming, and of the end of the world?

4 And Jesus answered and said unto them, Take heed that no man deceive you.

5 For many shall come in my name, saying, I am Christ; and shall deceive many.

6 And ye shall hear of wars and rumours of wars: see that ye be not troubled: for all *these things* must come to pass, but the end is not yet.

7 For nation shall rise against nation, and kingdom against kingdom: and there shall be famines, and pestilences, and earthquakes, in divers places.

8 All these *are* the beginning of sorrows.

9 Then shall they deliver you up to be afflicted, and shall kill you: and ye shall be hated of all nations for my name's sake.

10 And then shall many be offended, and shall betray one another, and shall hate one another.

11 And many false prophets shall rise, and shall deceive many.

12 And because iniquity shall abound, the love of many shall wax cold.

13 But he that shall endure unto the end, the same shall be saved.

14 And this gospel of the kingdom shall be preached in all the world for a witness unto all nations; and then shall the end come.

15 When ye therefore shall see the abomination of desolation, spoken of by Daniel the prophet, stand in the holy place, (whoso readeth, let him understand:)

16 Then let them which be in Judaea flee into the mountains:

17 Let him which is on the housetop not come down to take any thing out of his house:

18 Neither let him which is in the field return back to take his clothes.

19 And woe unto them that are with child, and to them that give suck in those days!

20 But pray ye that your flight be not in the winter, neither on the sabbath day:

21 For then shall be great tribulation, such as was not since the beginning of the world to this time, no, nor ever shall be.

22 And except those days should be shortened, there should no flesh be saved: but for the elect's sake those days shall be shortened.

23 Then if any man shall say unto you, Lo, here *is* Christ, or there; believe *it* not.

24 For there shall arise false Christs, and false prophets, and shall shew great signs and wonders; insomuch that, if *it were* possible, they shall deceive the very elect.

25 Behold, I have told you before.

26 Wherefore if they shall say unto you, Behold, he is in the desert; go not forth: behold, *he is* in the secret chambers; believe *it* not.

27 For as the lightning cometh out of the east, and shineth even unto the west; so shall also the coming of the Son of man be.

28 For wheresoever the carcase is, there will the eagles be gathered together.

29 Immediately after the tribulation of those days shall the sun be darkened, and the moon shall not give her light, and the stars shall fall from heaven, and the powers of the heavens shall be shaken:

30 And then shall appear the sign of the Son of man in heaven: and then shall all the tribes of the earth mourn, and they shall see the Son of man coming in the clouds of heaven with power and great glory.

31 And he shall send his angels with a great sound of a trumpet, and they shall gather together his elect from the four winds, from one end of heaven to the other.

32 Now learn a parable of the fig tree; When his branch is yet tender, and putteth forth leaves, ye know that summer *is* nigh:

33 So likewise ye, when ye shall see all these things, know that it is near, *even* at the doors.

34 Verily I say unto you, This generation shall not pass, till all these things be fulfilled.

35 Heaven and earth shall pass away, but my words shall not pass away.

36 But of that day and hour knoweth no *man*, no, not the angels of heaven, but my Father only.

37 But as the days of Noe *were*, so shall also the coming of the Son of man be.

38 For as in the days that were before the flood they were eating and drinking, marrying and giving in marriage, until the day that Noe entered into the ark,

39 And knew not until the flood came, and took them all away; so shall also the coming of the Son of man be.

40 Then shall two be in the field; the one shall be taken, and the other left.

41 Two *women shall be* grinding at the mill; the one shall be taken, and the other left.

42 Watch therefore: for ye know not what hour your Lord doth come.

43 But know this, that if the goodman of the house had known in what watch the thief would come, he would have watched, and would not have suffered his house to be broken up.

44 Therefore be ye also ready: for in such an hour as ye think not the Son of man cometh.

45 Who then is a faithful and wise servant, whom his lord hath made ruler over his household, to give them meat in due season?

46 Blessed *is* that servant, whom his lord when he cometh shall find so doing.

47 Verily I say unto you, That he shall make him ruler over all his goods.

48 But and if that evil servant shall say in his heart, My lord delayeth his coming;

49 And shall begin to smite *his* fellowservants, and to eat and drink with the drunken;

50 The lord of that servant shall come in a day when he looketh not for *him*, and in an hour that he is not aware of,

51 And shall cut him asunder, and appoint *him* his portion with the hypocrites: there shall be weeping and gnashing of teeth.

There are a number of things spoken about in Matthew 24. In this chapter I will be focusing on the separation part.

Jesus speaks of the Kingdom of Heaven in other parts of the Bible, but in this part he refers to it simply as "the kingdom", and how the gospel of this kingdom should be spread to the rest of this world.

He speaks of a sudden separation or bifurcation of the population.

From here we can infer three things:

1. There is more than one world. There is this corrupted world and there is a paradise world free of evil.

2. Sometime in the future there is a sudden separation, where some of the population will be in the corrupted world and some will end up in the paradise world. This paradise world is referred to as The Kingdom.

3. It is important that people are told not only about this paradise world, but that this corrupted world is not the only world.

When is this going to happen?

Why would God allow humans to live and die for thousands of years to only have this event where so few are saved at the end?

Also why would humans exist for thousands of years with almost no technological advancement until the last 200 years? Then there is a sudden rapid advancement of technology.

Back in 2014 when I had my experience, I believe I was perceiving what this rapture event entails. It has to do with freewill. People choose the path they are on by the choices they make in their life. This would explain why no one could be told when it will happen.

36. But of that day and hour knoweth no man, no, not the angels of heaven, but my Father only.

After this event some people will find themselves in a paradise world. In this world people have eternal life.
This event takes place in the future.

However, there is a past where humans live in a paradise world and have immortal life. Then legend has it humans started to age after eating from the tree of knowledge of good & evil. Their lifespans were about 5 to 10 times longer than the lifespans of humans today.
Living between 500 to 900 years on average, may sound great to someone in contemporary times, however to an immortal being, it would be short. Then after the great flood of Noah's time, lifespans were greatly reduced to what we have today.

So we are currently in a period between two perfect worlds. These two perfect worlds, the one in the past and the one in the future are separated by a wave. It is this wave that carries the chain of causality between the past and the future, and the wave flows in both directions. This is possible because that perfect world in the past and that perfect world in the future are the same world.

Part II

The Science

The Double Slit Experiment

What about the science?

Is there any scientific evidence for anything I have written about in this book so far?

Not only is there evidence from real observed science experiments, but also from the opposition themselves.

The first evidence that this is not the only world begins with the Double Slit experiment, first performed by Thomas Young in 1801.

Young shined light toward two slits and observed an interference pattern.

This experiment shows that light can display characteristics of both waves and particles. At that time it was thought that light consisted of either waves or particles.

Later in 1927 Clinton Davisson and Lester Germer, were working at what would later be called Bell Labs did a similar experiment. Except they used electrons that were scattered by the surface of nickel metal. This resulted in a similar diffraction pattern.
However, a true double slit experiment involving anything other than light did not take place until 1961 when Claus Jonsson performed it with electrons. This is evidence that the wave property of light extends to the macroscopic world as a whole.

Back in 1925 a man named Erwin Schrodinger formulated an equation to show how a matter wave should evolve.

Since matter and energy are the same thing, that is to say $E=mc^2$, we arrive at the conclusion that everything in this world we are perceiving is in a literal sense a holographic projection

My point being that what an individual perceives as solid matter is only a point on a deterministic wave moving at the speed of light. Both the individual and the solid matter he perceives (as solid), is because they are both moving at the same speed (relative to each other) in spacetime. This is a highly localized phenomenon. For example someone holding a paperback copy of this book in their hands will perceive this book as a solid object of matter, because they are directly in contact and very close along the slice of the deterministic wave function. When they put the book down and stand some distance way, even a few feet, they are no longer perceiving the book as a solid physical object. They are only perceiving the photons or light waves moving from the surface of the book to the retina of the eye.

The fundamental principle of this is something known as cause & effect. It is the principle of cause & effect that is the reason everyone in the room looking at the book will see the same thing. Or to put it another way, if someone speaks their vocal cords will cause atoms and molecules in the air to vibrate in a deterministic way from their mouth, thereby delivering the same basic pattern of information to the ears of everyone in the room.

So we have established that sound waves and light waves are the observed evidence that cause & effect is a fundamental principle of existence. Hence light waves or photons move at the maximum speed possible between the surface of the book and the retina of the reader, the speed of causality, this is the "c" in the equation $E=mc^2$. Energy of matter is the mass of it multiplied by the speed of causality squared. Everything is moving through time at the speed of causality, not just light. This is because everything is part of the wave function in Schrodinger's equation:

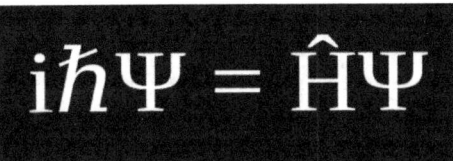

Back to the double slit experiment. It is observed that when photons are sent toward a target of 2 slits they will form an interference pattern on the wall behind the slits.

It would appear as if the light was passing through both slits simultaneously and interfering with itself forming an interference pattern on the wall. However, something strange happens when an attempt is made to observe which of the two slits a single photon passes through.

When photo detectors are placed at each of the slits to detect which of the slits the photons are passing through, the interference pattern disappears and we are left with 2 spots along the wall where the photons are hitting.

It would appear that the photons change their behavior based on whether a detector is there to watch them pass through the slits. It is like the photons are consciously aware of being watched.

How could this be?

The only way this can be without violating the fundamental precept of cause & effect is if there are simultaneous historic paths of the photons, and each are equally real. This is the scientific evidence that parallel or multiple worlds exist. These results also confirm the validity of Schrodinger's equation showing that everything is moving at a deterministic wave function. In fact it was Erwin Schrodinger himself who first spoke about how multiple worlds must exist and be equally real. Each world would appear as the most real world to the entities inhabiting it.

The Copenhagen Deception

"Humpty Dumpty sat on a wall,
Humpty Dumpty had a great fall;
All the King's horses
And all the King's men,
Couldn't put Humpty together again."

In the last chapter I wrote about how there is scientific evidence that this is not the only world. This is backed by Schrodinger's work, as well as others.

However, there was a group that met in Copenhagen to oppose this. The two most famous of these are Werner Heisenberg and Niels Bohr. It was Werner Heisenberg where the term "Copenhagen interpretation" was originated from, based on a lose translation from his native language.

Heisenberg's book "The Physical Principles of Quantum Theory" was published in 1930. In it he used the term "Kopenhagener Geist der Quantentheorie" translated into English as "Copenhagen spirit of quantum theory", later people would paraphrase it as simply the Copenhagen interpretation.

The Copenhagen interpretation throws causality out the window by arguing for an indeterministic quantum mechanics, thereby contradicting Schrodinger's equation of a deterministic wave function. Heisenberg attempts to do this by replacing it with his home brew "matrix mechanics" and "uncertainty principle".

After examining this Copenhagen interpretation, and having conversations over the years with its defenders, it appears to be an attempt to hobble together a logical incoherent argument that this is the only world. Not only does it break the fundamental principle of cause & effect, but it actually breaks the possibility of objective freewill.

Objective freewill defined, is the possibility to do otherwise.

For objective freewill to exist, then the possibility to do otherwise must exist and be equally real. Schrodinger's deterministic wave function equations points to this as well as the results of the double slit experiments conducted. Werner Heisenberg's Copenhagen interpretation does the opposite.

This begs the question:

Why would someone or group do such a sophisticated attack on the concept of objective freewill?

Que Bono? i. e. Who benefits?

The answer is obvious.

As I have written at the beginning of this book. They prefer the world the way it is. They crave a world of masters and slaves, and they intend to be the masters. They are bureaucrats and arrogant managers on power trips. Their highest desire is to push people around. If their victims knew that this was not the only world, they would be more inclined to push back.

This is the reason why the establishment institutions controlled by the demonic rulers of this world pushed the most illogical and incoherent interpretation of quantum mechanics through their universities and media propaganda outlets to the general population, for almost a century.

Also, the Copenhagen interpretation does not just break objective freewill. It appears to create a world where "freewill" is unequally bestowed on the upper classes (i.e. the rulers of this world). It also reduces or eliminates the freewill of everyone else in the system. It does not really do these things objectively, it is the argument that the ruling class use to deceive the working class into accepting the yoke of bondage. This is just a more recent re-branding of the "Divine right to rule" by royalty. Now they call themselves such things as "the Elite", or "the Educated".

Schrodinger's Cat

"The task is ... not so much to see what no one has yet seen; but to think what nobody has yet thought, about that which everybody sees."
— Erwin Schrodinger

Many have heard or read about Schrodinger's Cat.
I would wager that most of those people don't know that Erwin Schrodinger's famous thought experiment with the cat was him actually arguing against the Copenhagen Interpretation.

This is a hypothetical experiment where a cat is placed into a box or cage. Along with the cat, the cage also contains a sealed container of poison. There is a device that measures the decay of a radioactive substance. According to historical observations, this radioactive substance has a 50% probability of decaying in a certain time frame. If the substance decays in the time frame, the detector will trigger a hammer to break open the container of poison, thereby killing the cat. According to the Copenhagen interpretation of quantum mechanics, the cat will be simultaneously alive and dead up until the moment the box is opened and the scientists looks into the box. Then by some unknown magic or "hidden variable" the simultaneous alive and dead state of the cat will collapse into one state of either alive or dead. This is referred to as collapse of the wave.

But what about the cat?

Isn't the cat also an observer?

If according to the Copenhagen interpretation the involvement of an observer collapses a superposition of simultaneous states into one, then a human observer would not be special. That is to say, the cat is also an observer.

But if the cat is an observer, and the quantum system requires the involvement of an observer, then from the cat's perspective, the poison will never be released. For if the poison is released and the cat dies, then the cat is no longer an involved observer.

The only way to resolve this paradoxical situation is for the existence of more than one actual real worlds.
In fact there would be an increasing number of worlds going forward in time where the poison was being released, and there would always be at least one world where the cat is alive.

The Theory of the Universal Wave Function

"Since the universal validity of the state function description is asserted, one can regard the state functions themselves as the fundamental entities, and one can even consider the state function of the entire universe. In this sense this theory can be called the theory of the "universal wave function," since all of physics is presumed to follow from this function alone" - Hugh Everett , The Theory of the Universal Wave Function 1956

The first logical consistent interpretation of quantum mechanics is contained in Hugh Everett's PhD thesis originally titled The Theory of the Universal Wave Function.

This would later be called the "relative state interpretation" of quantum mechanics, or more commonly known as the many worlds interpretation.

Here I will attempt to put my interpretation of the Theory of the Universal Wave Function, as well as what it implies.

Hugh Everett's theory is the only one that is consistent with both classical physics and quantum mechanics (AKA quantum physics). It also does not break CPT symmetry, while the Copenhagen interpretation does break CPT symmetry.

CPT symmetry is short for Charge, Parity, Time reversal symmetry. The CPT theorem says that CPT symmetry holds for all physical phenomena. Hence, a mirror image of our universe, with all positions and momentum reversed, and all matter replaced by antimatter, would follow the exact same deterministic history.

The mirror image is in a literal sense, the other side of a wave.

When I was a young child, I had the opportunity to visit a carnival. There was all kinds of grifters and hustlers. Someone would offer to guess people's ages and weight for a price. There were all sort of rigged games to play. However, what I remember after all those years was a house of twisted mirrors.

I walked into this building that was filled with mirrors, and I noticed that in each of the mirrors, my reflection, **the image of me**, was distorted. Each mirror reflected back its own unique distorted image.

What is my point?

My point was to conceptualize an idea.

It is simply this:
The foundation of existence is the very essence of perfection itself. All worlds outside of this perfect world, are in varying degrees of distortion, relative to the distance from that state of perfection, it finds itself along the wave function. These are the many worlds of the Hugh Everett interpretation. I believe this is also why he later called his theory the "relative state interpretation".
This perfect world would have no motion, and would be in a state of zero entropy. All imperfect worlds are simply holographic projections from that perfect world. Also this perfect world is timeless. That is to say time only exists in the imperfect worlds. From the point of view of those of us in an imperfect world, the perfect world exists outside or at the end of time.
Each of us exist as a part of the wave function. As such each individual being has objective freewill.

Part of the scientific method is the concept of Falsifiability, i. e. a theory is falsifiable (or refutable).
An example of a theory that is falsifiable is to say that there is no such thing as a cat with green fur. Since it at any time in the

future, the discovery of a cat with green fur, will refute the statement. However, the statement that there is no such thing as a cat with green fur, remains true as long as no cats with green fur are ever observed.

Parallel universes are not a theory in themselves, but a prediction of Hugh Everett's Theory of the Universal Wave Function.
For a theory to be falsifiable, we need not observe and test all its predictions, one will do.
Hugh Everett's theory is falsifiable by future lab experiments.

The Copenhagen Interpretation is inherently constructed as an unfalsifiable one. The defenders of the Copenhagen Deception will always move the goal posts in defense of their deception.

One of their arguments against the many worlds interpretation, is a violation of the law of conservation of energy. They claim that the constant spitting of worlds would require an increase in energy and mass going into the future. However, the Universal Wave Function is at its core time symmetric. The concept of worlds splitting is a consequence of time linear thinking. Those worlds already exist objectively on their own. Also the splitting also referred to as decoherence would violate the symmetry of the wave function if they were irreversible.

The interference pattern alone, is observed evidence that the waves recombine after splitting and going through the slits simultaneously.
Some would ask where is the evidence of collisions or the merging of separate worlds ?

If there is decoherence, then symmetry requires a merger, or recoherence.

I would argue that there are mergers of worlds happening constantly just as there are splittings. These would add up to the point of canceling out any apparent violations of conservation of energy and mass.

Evidence of the merging is currently taking place in the energy patterns of the brains of individual observers.
Everything exists along the wave function, including the atoms and molecules that construct the neurons of the brains of the observers. Therefor, small scale mergers of the worlds would at first appear as having multiple sets of memories (See the chapter on the Mandela effect in the first part of this book).
Other evidence of the merger of worlds (waves) are:

Dreams of the future that later come true or even partially true in a distorted way.

Visions of the future or future events, that later come true.

Deja Vu

Precognition of any type.

Most of these things I touched on in the first part of this book. However, it was my twilight zone experience that set me on these years of research until I discovered Hugh Everett's work and saw how it was all connected. This is the reason why I included those things in part one of this book.

Then the ultimate question remains:

What would an observer or individual experience, if they observed a large scale merger of worlds, involving many observers simultaneously?

The Event

"In the universe, there are things that are known, and things that are unknown, and in between, there are doors." -William Blake

During my years of research, the phrase "The Event" started showing up in the language of the reports I was skimming through. At first I put all reports and sources using the phrase "The Event" in the circular file next to such things as ufoology. I did this because over the years of research I would find plenty of bullshit to sort through. Much of the bullshit was (and still is) put out by agents of the ruling class to distract and confuse people. (for example "Flat Earth")

One day I decided to take a closer examination of this thing people were calling "The Event".

In the first part of this book I referred to the real rulers of this world as simply the Precogs. These are the evil or negative Precogs.
I also spoke about how there are also good Precogs in a previous chapter titled "The Rapture". The latest reports I was examining appeared to contain information from good or positive Precogs speaking of something they were calling "The Event". Upon further research, I have come to the conclusion that this thing the good Precogs are calling "The Event" is closely related to something many are calling "The Rapture". These two things may be distinct events that are very close together on the wave function timeline, or they may in fact be the exact same thing.

Henceforth I will refer to either of these as simply "The Event", or "This Event".

One common theme that is in many of the reports from the good Precogs is the phrase "New Earth". I would also point out the phrase "New Earth" is specifically used by a famous Precog in the "Revelation of John the Divine", this is the last part of a book most would recognize as the Bible. This gives further weight to the idea that the Event and the Rapture are most likely the same thing.

So far all of the Precogs that put out a specific time frame for when this event will happen has failed as a prediction, as the date and/or time specified passed. In fact a more common theme among the Precogs is that this event is unpredictable. This includes a statement from one of the most famous Precogs Jesus when he said:

"But of that day and hour knoweth no man, no, not the angels of heaven, but my Father only."

I believe this Father he is referring to, is the being that set the wave function in motion out from the prefect world. Since we exist along the wave function, such a being who started it, would in fact be our ultimate parent.

At this point I will reiterate that it is not my intention to argue in favor of a particular religion. However, in researching this book and specifically the Universal Wave Function, I saw too many connections between many of the historical scriptures from the Bible, including many that are not included in the Bible, such as the Nag Hammadi texts, and the book of Enoch.

I will also point out that the Theory of the Universal Wave Function, is the only scientific interpretation of quantum mechanics compatible with all the events written about in the Biblical texts, including the existence of a heaven and a hell, along with everything in between.

I am also aware that the Council of Nicaea along with most organized religions are part of the deception, (i. e. the control system used by the demonic rulers of this world).

This begs the question:
Why bring up old Biblical and historical texts that are being used by varying degrees by those same groups that are opposing the only scientific theory that is compatible with those very texts?

It is simple, the greatest deceptions, are the ones that contain the most truth.

As an example, I'll tell the story of the evil genius (similar to the evil Precogs ruling this world today).

Long ago there was once an evil Precog, who knew in advance of a total solar eclipse going to happen directly over his village. He told the people of his village that he will make the sun go dark in the middle of the day. When this happened the people of his village got scared and asked him to bring the sun back. Of course he quickly agreed, with the stipulation that he be made King. When the eclipse ended they bowed before him, and made him King of the local tribe.

That is one example of a Precog, using his temporal advantage to rule over others.

While his reign is based on deception, it does not change the fact that the moon did come between the sun and the Earth, casting a shadow down on the local village.

My point is this:
While there are those using historical texts to create another control system, the fact remains that the texts in the Bible are based on the premise that this is not the only world, and there is a valid scientific theory that indicates this.

Ironically the author of that Theory, Hugh Everett, shows as an atheist or agnostic, in the historical record of this world.

But, why would the rulers of this world, want to push illogical scientific interpretations to deceive the people into believing that this is the only world that exists ?

I believe it is their rear guard action to delay or stop this Event from happening. In my research it would appear that the timeline on the wave function where we can merge with a better world is one that must be chosen freely, not only individually but also collectively.

Previously I wrote about how things like deja vu and other forms of precognition are the evidence of mergers between nearly identical worlds that are only slightly out of phase with each other. This is because the merger is happening at an individual brain structure. Then I ask the question, basically what a large scale merger between worlds that are significantly different look like? Especially if such a merger was experienced by many observers?

I believe that the Event, and/or Rapture is a large scale merger between worlds. I used to think that only what I do as an individual, would take me to that timeline. However, years of research and experimentation, would seem to indicate that this is also a group effort, as well as individual one. This will require cooperation among a certain portion of the population.
This is because such a paradise world is one of cooperation, so it would logically stand to reason that getting there would require some form of cooperation.

The spitting of worlds is taking place at decision points, both individually and collectively. This is known as decoherence. These alternative worlds exist as a consequence of objective freewill. While conversely, the merger of worlds (waves) is known as recoherence.

Now what is coherent light? It is a light beam where all the waves are aligned perfectly or nearly perfectly. This is also known as a laser beam. A laser can punch through, where non-coherent light cannot.

Each of us are part of the holographic projection, that is the wave function. Our bodies including our brains are made of this light wave, we only perceive ourselves and others as solid matter. My point being, that each of us are a wave, and when we cooperate, our light (our part of the wave function) becomes more coherent with each other. This coherence power increases exponentially as more people cooperate (the group is larger). This forms a powerful laser beam that will eventually be great enough to punch through the deception matrix constructed by the evil Precogs and their servants. It is this coherent power that will open the gates to the merger to a better world for those who are part of this coherent cooperation. When this happens there will be a separation, like the breaking of a rubber band, those who are part of the negative parasitical control system will snap back into a worse world.

This brings us back full circle to the chapter titled "The Rapture" in part one of this book, where I include the ext of Matthew 24.

Jesus speaks of this Event, and speaks about spreading the knowledge of this event to the population of the world. That is to say, "spreading the Gospel" in all the world. My analysis of the teachings of Jesus would indicate that:

He knew the scientific reality of existence.

He knew the inevitable consequence of objective freewill is that people will make mistakes (choose the wrong path along the wave function).

He spent the last years of his life teaching cooperation among people.

It is clear to me now that this teaching of cooperation and about the "narrow path" is about coherence, because it is cooperation and the narrow path that brings coherence among the people who seek a better world. However, he also taught that we should NOT cooperate with the enemy. Hence his talking about not being a "friend of the world" (i. e. This World)

I believe this is the real message of Jesus, and not the false control religion created by people like Paul (who appears in my analysis to be working to corrupt and twist the original message) and the council of Nicaea .

I also believe the reason why no one could be told when this event will take place, is because every timeline where people are told, the evil Precogs are able to sabotage and stop it from happening somehow.

Most of all I believe this is why the demonic rulers of this world have a special unwavering anger at Jesus, and any who attempt to follow his original teaching of cooperation. Because when enough of the population cooperates, their (the evil Precogs) temporal advantage will be eliminated.

Those of us who desire a world of justice must cooperate with each other to overcome the enemy, but we must have enough wisdom to recognize the enemy.

Because the enemy is using our desire for goodness, our kindness, are willingness to cooperate, and twist it. They have set up systems of deception where most good people are cooperating with our enemy, bring us to our destruction. While, conversely they have poisoned us against each other with an "every man for himself" competitive attitude. They have only got the good people to compete with other good people, not with the enemy, and the enemy does NOT compete among themselves.

They are coordinated and directed to such an extreme, they make the Borg in Star Trek, look like the 3 Stooges.

Who are the enemy?

Part III

Demonic Infiltration Strategy

The Adversary

"Anybody can become angry — that is easy, but to be angry with the right person and to the right degree and at the right time and for the right purpose, and in the right way — that is not within everybody's power and is not easy." — Aristotle

As I've mentioned before, this book is for the workers, the inventors, engineers, and true scientists.

Who am I talking about?

They are the producers of all the real wealth in the civilization. It is them that maintain the critical infrastructure like electric power, energy production. They are the farmers that work the fields, to produce the food. They work as factory workers to manufacture the products for civilization. They are the truck drivers and train engineers who transport the products produced by the farmers and factory workers. Above are examples of the working class.

Who is not a member of the working class?

All career direct out of college managers. Because any direct out of college manager was never part of the working class, and as such has no business lecturing the worker about laziness. Any career government employee. This also includes all law enforcement, because the very concept of career full time professional law enforcement is repugnant to the concept of a Republic that serves the people.

The only college educated professionals, that I would count as working class are people like engineers, and other "STEM" fields, IF the position they are working in is related to production, and/or maintaining the infrastructure.

Earlier in this book, I wrote about the Precogs. Both evil Precogs and good Precogs. At the time of this writing the evil Precogs are in the dominate position of the Earth. The good Precogs are disorganized and while there are some public good Precogs, most are in hiding or are operating "below the radar". The evil Precogs recognize the good Precogs as a threat to their power monopoly, so they regularly will attempt to buy off the good Precogs with extra money and/or positions of rank within the evil Precogs power monopoly. If they can't buy off the good Precog they will attempt things like blackmail, and other threats, up to including assassination.

The main tools of the evil Precogs are the managerial class, and the government bureaucrats, mainly law enforcement. They have used these tools to enslave the workers. Their system of deception is so effective that most of the slaves are under the delusion that they are free.

I wrote at the beginning of this book about exposing the cheat code, and explaining the real secret. To do this I must first start in a time when briefly , the good Precogs were the dominate group, not on Earth as a whole, but in a part of North America in the late 1700's to early 1800's. There are few times in the history of this world where I can find a record of the good Precogs removing and breaking the evil Precogs power monopoly.

The last time the good Precogs were organized, they started events in motion, to commence 1776.

Unfortunately they were not successful in totally removing the evil Precogs from influence. They compromised with the evil Precogs to allow slavery in the southern states among other things. Still that little bit of real Liberty that was won in the late 1700's led to a nation where for a time, the working class had the highest standard of living and freedom on the planet.

The King of France saw the good Precogs success in the newly formed united States of America and began the process of dismantling the local evil Precog power monopoly in France. It was the evil Precogs and the managerial class in France who started the fake French revolution, NOT the lower working class of France. It was the evil Precogs who stopped the King of France from giving the people (the workers) real freedom.

What is the goal of the evil Precogs?

Evidence from my research, indicates that the evil Precogs are being directed and guided by the interdimensional beings I shall refer to simply as Demonics.

The evil Precogs appear to be guided to enslave the rest of the human race. This enslavement is accomplish by a number of tools they employ.

The Time Travelers

Many of the evil Precogs have referred to themselves as a Traveling Man, or in public as "Fellow Travelers".

As I have stated in the previous chapter "The Adversary". There was a time in the late 1770's that good Precogs founded the united States of America. They knew what was going to happen, even George Washington had a vision of the future that involved a number of wars, with a final battle that appears to be close enough on the timeline (as I write this) to be within a few years away at the most. Some would argue that this war has already started. It also showed up in my research, the George Washington, warned of the evil Precogs infiltrating the lodges, shortly before his death.

Decades ago when I was a young man, I considered for a time, joining the Blue Lodge. Even though I am not an initiate of any lodge, I will refer to myself as a Traveling Man. I do this to take back the title because it belonged to the good Precogs long before the lodges got corrupted by the evil Precogs.

For some reason many of the good Precogs will see the Adversary start to use a phrase or song and will surrender it. Then many in our side stop using the phrase, song or symbol, because they are too cowardly to defend it. This is one of the biggest tools they Adversary has used to gain power, as the good surrender territory, to them.

There are a number of other tools they employ such as:

Setting up central banks.

Giving a club they control a monopoly authority over all the working of the courts in almost every State in the united States. They did this by amending almost every State constitution starting in the mid to late 1800's to include language requiring someone to be a member of the BAR before they could sit as a Judge in the court or defend the accused in court. They still have not amended the constitution of the United States of America to require someone on the federal court to be a member of the BAR. It is possible for a President to nominate someone who is not a member of the BAR to be on any federal court even the supreme court. Not likely as the last time we had anything resembling a free election for President was in 2016.

Formation of capital pools also known as "Private Equity" or sometimes hedge funds. This is just a re-branding of the controlling "Trusts" that they set up over 100 years ago. This is where we get the term "anti-trust" or anti-trust legislation, because the people (and some good Precogs) started to oppose and resist the Adversary buying up all the companies and land in the USA through the use of Trusts. They have simply re-branded to "Private Equity" and are doing the same thing.

Buying up all daily newspapers in the USA. In my research I saw how there is less than 5 capital pools also know as private equity that control or have controlling interest in every daily newspaper in the USA.

Setting up Business schools to install a royal class of managers, to oversee the dismantling of all free enterprise, or all fee markets. They did this slowly while maintaining the illusion of a fee market. This is in tandem with their capital pools.

Taking over all Non-Profit hospitals and using them as weapons of destruction against the middle and working class population of the USA

Setting up standing armies in every State starting over 100 years ago. In most states they are referred to as State Police.

These are just a few of the main tools they employ.

They use their control of media to wage psychological warfare against the population.

Mistakes of the Founders of the USA

Most would agree that compromising and allowing slavery to continue in the southern states of the USA was a huge mistake, that allowed the Demonics to get a foothold in the USA. This led to a civil war mainly engineered by an evil Precog named Albert Pike. It was also Albert Pike who completed the demonic takeover of the lodges in the USA. He did this under the direction of the demonic English monarchy.

Another mistake they made was in copying the monarchy's royal system of control of the military, by instituting a direct commissioned officer class in the military.

The united States of America was supposed to be a Republic by and for the people. If the people are meant to be the ultimate masters, then having a military commanded by direct commissioned officers is an abomination.

No one should be allowed to be commissioned an officer until after they have served at least two years in the enlisted ranks.

Having no constitutional process whereby an individual state can peaceably leave the union. There is a part of the constitution proscribing the procedures whereby a territory of state can join the union, but nowhere is is written how they can leave.

Psychological Warfare

There are a number of ways they are waging psychological warfare against the people. They use a sophisticated form of deception. They also rely on members of target population having a short memory.

They use a coordinated attack of shills along with their media assets to carry out the deception. I call this "the devil's matrix speaking" or "the devil's matrix speaks".

They do this about events or if people are talking about a situation or event, especially in an online forum.

For example :

I saw reports come across my desk over the years about a volcano in the canary islands being a possible threat of a tsunami. Then I saw an increase of reports in August of 2021 about a volcano erupting and causing a tsunami. Some of the older reports were from media assets controlled by The Devil's Matrix. I didn't have an opinion of if a volcano in the canary islands could cause a tsunami. However, after the volcano started erupting in September 2021, I saw The Devil's Matrix start to speak in contradiction of what it had spoken years before.

First they put out the narrative that a volcano in the canary islands could not cause a tsunami.

Then they started talking about the mere idea that a volcano or Earthquake could cause a large tsunami as crazy conspiracy theory and crackpot science. This is an example of their deception relying on people having short memories. There were 2 large tsunamis caused by earthquakes within the last 20 years. The December 2004 tsunami and then the 2011 tsunami.

When The Devil's Matrix puts resources into convincing people into not looking at something, look at it.

Another deception they use is to conceal or obfuscate the use of force or coercion.

Responding to being treated unfairly to the working class with "no one is pointing a gun at your head".
There are many guns being pointed at the working class heads. Lets start with law enforcement. These are the modern day taskmasters of Egypt. When a worker stops working, eventually law enforcement will show up where he lives. Unless he stopped working because he won the lottery. Of course that only keeps the taskmaster with guns from showing up because he has money to pay them off (taxes).

A free people are never told they are free. Nor do they need to be.

"Police don't write laws, if you don't like the law you should vote to change the law." I went to a state capitol and saw there were actual police officers telling the legislature what to pass. They were always asking for more powers, more immunity, etc.

The USA is the main target of the evil Precogs, because the USA was founded by the good Precogs to fight as a weapon against the evil Precogs and their demonic master's plans to enslave and destroy the human race. One main thing that had to do was shut down as much local manufacturing as they could. They used their business schools they set up in the late 1880s along with private equity capital pools to accomplish this objective.

   They used their media assets they control to put out the deceptive narrative that the reason the factory were being moved to countries outside the USA was because "the American consumer choose to buy foreign goods"

or

"the American consumer does not choose to buy Made in the USA goods"

This is a deception put out by people who aren't old enough to remember how it happened, or people who don't have a functional long term memory. I was born in the 1970's and I am old enough to remember how things happened. I remember that in the mid to late 1980s, with the exception of some electronics from Japan, almost everything being Made in the USA.

   Then in the late 1980s until the early 1990s I saw more stuff showing up on the store shelves from other countries outside the USA. I also saw and heard people talking about how they would not by stuff from other nations, especially clothes. People seemed to accept electronics first. But up until the early 1990s almost all clothes were Made in the USA. I remember watching a news story on the controlled media about how Americans were choosing to buy Made in the USA clothes almost exclusively, even though the clothes from outside the USA on the store selves were cheaper.

It wasn't long after that, perhaps a year or 2 when every clothes manufacture in the USA announced almost simultaneously within months of each other, that they are closing their factory in the USA and moving production to south east Asia, mainly China.

The evil Precogs thru the appointment of executive stooges from their business schools did this, NOT the American consumer.

Over the decades since, I've watched the evil Precogs infiltrate almost any corporation that owns any manufacturing facility in the USA and begin to sabotage it. If they can't get their people in positions of management in a factory, they will use their Private Equity (capital pools, hedge funds etc) to purchase it outright or do some hostile takeover leverage buyout scheme. After the takeover, they will sometimes announce through the media that they control, that the factory is to be closed and all production is being moved to China.

This was recently done with a Baseball bat factory. If they don't close the factory immediately it is because they are going to take a few years sabotaging the operations.

All recessions, were pre-planned by the Evil Precogs and implemented by their managerial class. They do this regularly every few years, as a mechanism to keep the working class in their place as slaves.

What is slavery?

The Difference between Freedom and Slavery

"Only free men can negotiate; prisoners cannot enter into contracts. Your freedom and mine cannot be separated." - Nelson Mandela

When people complain about being treated unfairly, the Devil's Matrix will eventually respond with "it's a free market, THEY have the right do whatever they want." In this context, "THEY" is never a member of the working class. "THEY" is a rich person, or corporate executive. Because the Devil's Matrix only speaks in defense of the predators.

This deception has its inception, by the deliberate inversion, of what a "right" is.

For most of us, individual rights, are about being free from, or being able to take action to defend ourselves against predators.

The predators definition of a right, is about being able to feed on their victims, unhindered. For example, in the movie Braveheart , one of the ruling class predators, rides into the village and announces he will be taking the man's new wife into his bed on their wedding night. He claims it is his "right", to do so.

Now, notice what happens, when a working class man walks down the street exercising his "right" to defend himself from predators. In a large percentage of the world, a man walking down the street, with a revolver strapped to his waist in a holster, will be immediately set upon by predators wearing a costume (AKA a uniform).

The evil Precogs infiltrated and directed the governments of the world, through legislation and judicial rulings to almost totally annihilate the individual right of the people to defend themselves against the predators. This is because the evil Precogs are working for and being directed by the Demonics.

There are a few place where the human population still retain some legal right to defend themselves from predators, (such as the united States) however even in these places, that right, is extremely restricted.

What is a free market?

To define a free market, we must first define, what is freedom.

Many years ago, I watched a movie, about a man who was the sole survivor of a plane crash. Apparently he was some big corporate manager or executive at a transportation company. In the movie, he is alone on an island.

On this island where he is the only human, a life free from coercion exists without question.

He alone is responsible for his survival.

He alone will face the consequences of any choice he makes.

He will bear the cost of all action or inaction he takes.

If he does not fish, or farm, or hunt, he will starve.

In this place the concept of lazy or laziness does not exist. This is true in any place where humans are free from coercion.

The very premise behind word "lazy", only exists in a world of masters and slaves, and it is a word used most often by those who intend to be the masters.

Now, if we add a second man to this hypothetical island, then there is now the possibility of fraud (deception), and/or coercion (i. e. violence, or threat of violence).

Hence, when there is more than one human, there is both opportunity for mutual cooperation, where everyone's standard of living (survival) is raised, and the possibility of predatory or master – slave situation, where one person or group's standard of living is raised at the cost of lowering the others. This is called injustice, or inequity.

The true free market way for more than one human to interact is by agreement, also known as contract. The fisherman agrees to trade a number of fish in exchange for a number of coconuts harvested by the other human.

The problem arises when people break their word (i. e. break the contract). For what is a contract, but an agreement that two or more parties will keep their word.

There are only two ways humans can interact with each other, by contract, or by coercion.

For a contract to be valid all parties must have freely agreed to it, with the choice to not enter into the contract if the other side is unwilling to negotiate.

The alternative is slavery, because the slave is unable to walkaway, and the master is unwilling to negotiate.

In a true objective free market, there is always a contract involving all market interactions. These may not always be a written contract. The contract may be verbal only, or "implied".

To make the statement in a market interaction :

"There is no contract, implied or otherwise", is to say, *"this is a Master – Slave interaction, and I intend to be the Master"*.

Among free humans, the only remedy to hold the man who breaks his word, is retaliation (i. e. negative consequences).

It has long been a custom to delegate the right to retaliate to a neutral or impartial mediator or group of mediators. This started in the ancient days, with disputes being handed by a tribal council.

In more recent contemporary times, the disputes involving breech of contract are decided in courtrooms by judges and in some cases, by juries.

This is the original reason courts were established.

If there is to be a set of laws or "rulebook", then everyone should have the absolute right to cite the "rulebook" in his defense.

The first sign of an authoritarian tyranny is the argument by the upper class, (the rich), that the working class should not have the right to cite the rulebook. The moment the rulebook does not apply equally to both the janitor and the manager, the free market has been replaced with a fascist police state.

A wise man once said, *"behind every double standard is a single standard."*

I would argue that behind every double standard involving the rulebook, is the standard of slavery.

As I have mentioned previously in this book, the united States of America was founded by the good Precogs. Until the late 1870s a working class man had the absolute right to ask that the rulebook be applied to a wealthy man who broke his word (i. e. breech of contract), or treated the working class in a dishonest way (i. e. fraud).
The rich predatory class directed by the resurgence of the evil Precogs (and the Demonics), in the mid 1800s were annoyed with having to deal with the working class in the courts.

While the rich Biff controlled businesses became more belligerent toward the working class population in the mid to late 1800s, there was a response by the working class to seek justice in the courts. Many of the courts in the 1800s still had a neutral position on the right of contract. That is to say the courts were equally inclined to hold a manager to his word as well as a janitor.

Now that is a free market, not today where the courts will hold a janitor to his word, but when the working man seeks to have the manager keep his word, we are told "he can do whatever he wants, its a free market"

See how that deception works ?

The biggest major response by the Demonics and the evil Precog minions (i. e. Biffs), was an argument started by the agent Horace (G or C) Wood. In 1877 the Demonic agent Mr Wood published his deception titled Master & Servant. For some reason he did not go all the way and call it Master & Slave). The Biffs of this word have used it to argue that the working class does not have contract rights, or that they (the managers) do not have to keep their word with a member of the working class.

Eventually the corporate managers were able to convince the courts to create the double standard we have today, where working class employees are subject to arbitrary whims of managers and corporate executives.

This is known as "at will" employment or "employment at will".

Tribal

In my research of the history of free or relatively free people coexisting together, the most stable organization I could find was called a Tribe or collection of Tribes called a confederation or confederacy.

I will use the word tribe instead of community, for the following reason:

The word community in place of tribe has been twisted in part of a language deception, that allowed the predators to infiltrate and corrupt the tribe. They used it to create words like communism and society, thereby inverting the traditional tribal loyalty to the tribe, into loyalty to the predators (i. e. loyalty to society).

This is also how they divided the tribe and caused members of the tribe to turn against other members of the tribe.

The word "society" is also a code word they use to refer to themselves. This is the ruling predator class openly claiming themselves as Masters and the rest of humanity as slaves they own.

Whenever you read their media propaganda, replace all instances of the word "society" with "the ruling class" or "our masters" and it fits perfectly.

The evil Precogs were able to look over the time horizon and see how tribal loyalty was one of the biggest if not the biggest impediment to their plans to enslave then exterminate the human race. This is why they admit in their own white papers that tribal loyalty is a problem for them.

In a truly objectively free, tribe, all adult members of the tribe have the absolute right and the duty to defend the tribe against outside predators. This was true whether the predators walked on four legs or two legs.

Infiltration of the Tribe

The evil Precog's most successful attack on the tribe was getting them to accept taskmasters appointed among them. They deceived the members of the tribe to sell them and their descendant's right to defend their tribe to a full time "professional defense force". With this great deception they were able to get the tribe to surrender their freedom, to the predators. The taskmasters they appointed are called Law Enforcement. From that time forward the wealth of the tribe will be increasingly transferred from the general population of the tribal members to a handful of predators and their mercenary forces.

Did you ever notice how the areas with the most taskmasters have the most crime?

To enslave and eventually exterminate a people, first loyalty to other members of the Tribe must be broken.
They accomplish this by turning the tribal loyalty against itself. To put it another way, they "take advantage of our kindness". They find any type of naivety of the tribal members to exploit.

What do I mean by "Tribal loyalty" or "loyalty to the other members of the Tribe"?

When a member of the tribe is in trouble, there is almost an inescapable compelling instinct to help them, experienced by other members of the tribe.
They subconsciously know that if they were in trouble, they would want or need others to come to their defense or aid.

One such example of infiltration, in more contemporary times, is the rich men dressing down then standing at busy roads, holding up cardboard signs, asking for aid. These rich (or relatively wealthy by others of magnitude above working class men), saw the tribal instinct to help another member of the tribe in trouble.

At that point, the rich man, took off his nice clothes, parked his Cadillac Escalade, put on some old torn working class clothes and then pretended to be a member of the tribe, so he could infiltrate and steal from the tribe by deception.

He does not do this because he needs the money. He does this to hurt the tribe, and to teach them, (when his fraud is discovered), to not help others of the tribe, who need it.

The infiltrators, do this in a number of ways. It is not just about money. They also infiltrate to deceive and manipulate.

In ancient times, the tribe would learn to avoid danger. This led to a desire to communicate among other members of the tribe.
For example, a human may eat poison berries then later become sick, or worse die. They and/or the living witnesses would tell the other members of the tribe, not to eat those berries again. Tribal members would also communicate among themselves about the dangers of predators.

The most modern example of this warning communication, is in the form of ratings or "star ratings" (i. e. 5 stars perfect rating), about businesses or products. Before the internet rating system, people would talk in person or by telephone about good or bad food at a restaurant, for example.

One type of infiltration of the working class, by the managerial class, is befriending us, to then pretend to be us, while attacking our loyalty to each other. I spoke to a few of these infiltrators over the years, in person, and also did analysis of some of the online infiltrators (AKA internet social media shills). The ones I know in person would at first act like there was some loyalty, but then I noticed a pattern. When I would try to warn them about the dangers of predators who are preying on the working class (through a form of tribal communication a written about above), they would shift like Agent Smith and suddenly become a defense attorney of the outside predator. Over the years, many times I would spend time finding out who the online shills were, and to this day, I haven't discovered a blue collar working class man among them. Of course the ones I spoke to, in person had zero experience as a blue collar worker.

The tribal unit is something that existed in humanity's past, and it will exist again as the primary organization in humanity's future, if humanity has one.

The Mistake of assuming common ground with Evil

They walk among us, but they are NOT us.

In the previous chapter, I wrote about how the predators infiltrate the tribe to corrupt and enslave the people. I touched on how they use our own kindness against us.

I would argue that one of the most critical mistakes, members of the tribe make, is to assume common ground with our predatory infiltrators who pretend to be with us. I was thinking about how to explain their deception in words, when in my research, I discovered a quote put out on the internet years ago.

"The sinking of the Titanic was a miracle, for the lobsters in the ship's kitchen."

Now, let's put aside all the pedantic arguments about whether there were still lobsters in tanks on board, and if they could survive at the location the ship sank. For the purpose of this writing, lets assume that there were living lobsters, who escaped the ship when it sank, and lived a long life as free lobsters. We could even assume they lived a short life as free lobsters. The point being, they were able to know what true freedom was, before the end of their earthly lives in this world.

Now imagine the people on the ship were able to somehow communicate with the lobsters, on their level. Imagine some of the people putting on lobster costumes, and pretending to have a common long term interest with the lobsters.

Consider carefully the following question:

How foolish would the lobsters be, to pray for the health and well being, of the Titanic?

My point is this:

The predators are using the power that the members of the tribe have as our birthright, as a weapon, against the tribe itself., to enslave the tribe. We are at the point when they have deceived numerous members of the tribe to pray for the continuation of our enslavement, and eventual extermination. The two main ways this has happened is:

1: There is a tendency to assume common ground with people who we consider to be "fellow humans," members of our tribe.

2: The predators, knowing this, pretend to be us.

They walk among us, but they are NOT us.

Just as the sinking of the Titanic was a disaster for the people who were going to eat the lobsters, there are things that would be disasters for the predators, who prey on humans.

As I write these words, at this very moment, there is a system of enslavement and extermination on Earth. That system was built by the minions of the predators, under the direction of the evil Precogs. This system was originally funded, and financed by the evil Precogs' temporal advantage. The foundation of this system is control of media propaganda networks. It is those media propaganda networks that greatly magnify the capability of the predators to infiltrate the tribes of this world.

That system, like any system, is subject to the laws of physics. It has its own weaknesses and vulnerabilities. There are a few ways this propaganda network can be broken. All of them are considered to be disasters for the predators.

1. An overwhelming and spontaneous attack from the population of the Earth against it. According to my research, this is the least likely, but the odds are greater than zero chance of it happening.

2. A series of earthquakes strong enough to silence the technological foundation of the demonic control system.

3. An asteroid impact that would indirectly and/or directly cause #2.

4. A strong enough solar flare could silence their propaganda network and bring down large parts of the demonic control system. This solar flare, or series of flares, can have the added bonus of causing #2 to happen.

Everything on the above list, in addition to being a disaster for the predators, would also cause discomfort for a large percentage of the tribes of this world.

Continuing with the lobsters analogy, let's assume there were 100 lobsters in tanks when the Titanic hit the iceberg. Then for the sake of this hypothetical situation, we shall also assume about 90 lobsters survive the sinking of the Titanic and taste freedom, as free lobsters.

The predatory deception would use the death of the 10 lobsters to argue that the sinking of the Titanic was bad for the lobsters, because it cost them 10 percent of their population.

"We are all in this together, fellow lobsters, you wouldn't want anyone to get hurt?"

This is a deceptive reasoning. If the Titanic did not hit the iceberg, then 100 percent of the lobsters would be dead. From a pure logical point of view, the sinking of the Titanic did not cost the lobsters anything. On the contrary, it was a net improvement to the lobster's future, even of 90 percent of them did not survive the sinking of the Titanic.

The reasons listed in this chapter, are not the only things, that can bring down the demonic control system. I will discuss them, in the next chapter because I am unsure if they would result in discomfort for members of the tribes of the working class.

Unknowns

"Reports that say that something hasn't happened are always interesting to me, because as we know, there are known knowns; there are things we know we know. We also know there are known unknowns; that is to say we know there are some things we do not know. But there are also unknown unknowns—the ones we don't know we don't know." - *Donald Rumsfeld*

In the last chapter I wrote about possible future events that could bring down the demonic control system. The main point of the last chapter was to construct a logical argument that those events should not be feared or prayed against. I say this because if the demonic control system is not broken, then it will lead to the total enslavement, and eventual extinction, of the human race on Earth.

There are other events, that may not lead to discomfort or harm to a portion of the tribes of free humanity, while bringing down the demonic control system. These can be categorized as known unknowns, or unknown unknowns, depending on your point of view.

1. Magnetic Pole Reversal. This is an event that hasn't happened on Earth for over 700,000 years. Although there is evidence of a partial or incomplete reversal happening about 42,000 years ago. It is not known how this will affect, humanity on Earth. It is speculated that this magnetic reversal could interrupt the demonic interdimensional transmission, that is influencing the evil Precogs in this world. At this point a magnetic reversal can be classified as having both known unknowns and unknown unknown effects upon the future of humanity on Earth.

2. Alien invasion or intervention. Like the magnetic reversal, this contains known unknowns, and unknown unknowns.

There may or may not be other, events that could bring down the demonic control system, and free humanity from their enslavement. Such things I will put here simply as unknown unknowns.

There is one other thing that can bring down the demonic control system and free humanity. It is the one thing I am sure about. It is also the reason for the title of this book, for it is the thing, the evil Precogs and their demonic masters fear the most. I call this "The Failsafe."

The Failsafe

*"The tyrant dies and his rule is over, the martyr dies and his rule begins."-
Soren Kierkegaard*

If you made it this far, you might be asking why?

Why, the need for parallel worlds, at all?

Why can't there be just one or more perfect worlds?

Or if there has to be multiple worlds, why can't they all be paradise worlds?

Why the need for these hellish dystopian worlds to exist?

Why the apparent need for death?

Throughout this book I wrote about the problem of the Demonics, and the evil Precogs. These are parasites. The thing about parasites and predators, is they have to win. That is to say, there is no such thing as coexisting with them in the objective sense, or any logical sense at all. They exist as the inevitable consequence of freewill and causality. Once they came into existence they could not be destroyed without breaking causality or freewill. Hence the only way to protect the paradise worlds from being corrupted by the parasitical Demonics was the creation of the failsafe.

The mechanism that is used to quarantine the Demonics, is known by most lay people as TIME.   The paradise worlds are shielded by layers of time. This is indicated by the universal wave function, and Schrodinger's equation.

This is a perfect defense, because perfection could only be defended by perfection itself.

As I stated above the parasite has to win, to feed on our energy. Those of us who desire mutual cooperation and coexistence, have the advantage, in that we do not have to win outright.   Merely playing to a draw or stalemate, is enough to eventually starve the beast.

But if we existed in a paradise world in our past, why are we here in this Demonic parasite infested world?

The very purpose of the Copenhagen deception is to distract and conceal the existence from us of the failsafe. When we navigate the 4D maze of time, we escape, and we also remove our energy from the worlds inhabited by the Demonic parasites. This is the reason why the scientific institutions they control, continued to push the one world interpretation of quantum mechanics.

In my years of research, it is also indicated, that each of us must pass a test, and that part of passing this test is to learn the true structure of existence, and to choose good.   This has the effect of filtering out those who don't belong in the paradise worlds.   This is because those of us who live in one of these more hellish worlds, now know evil. For any of us to go to a paradise world without passing the test, would threaten that paradise world with corruption.   Those layers of time, that defend the paradise worlds from the Demonics also defended them from us who know evil. For, we had to know evil to learn how to defend the paradise worlds against the infiltration. The thing that we who pass the test gain from the Demonics and their evil Precog servants, is WISDOM.

As I have written before TANSTAAFL:

There are no free lunches. The Demonics do not get our energy for free. We gain in wisdom.

It is clear to me now, that it is impossible for a being to choose between good and evil without the existence of parallel worlds. A multiverse would need to be literally real in every sense.

For there to be the possibility of redemption or salvation, then the possibility must also exist to shift one's own Consciousness or soul, across the timelines.

There may be multiple ways the individual being experiences this shift across the timelines. As I have discussed part of it previously in this book, it bears repeating for emphasis.

1. Dreaming of events that later come true either partially or completely.

2. Experiences of Deja Vu

3. Any form of precognition.

The evil Precogs know of this power. This is the power they used to become rulers of this world. How else could a tiny percentage of the population seem to have an almost magically invincible iron grip over the rest of the population of humanity ?

There is however, no free lunch, not in this world, nor any other. The evil Precogs deceived the world, but they themselves are being deceived by the Demonics. The Demonics tricked them into using this power for evil. The price the evil Precogs pay, is that continued use of this power to serve the Demonics, brings them closer to the world of the Demonics. The abuse and torture they will eventually face from the Demonics is much greater then they have inflicted on the tribes of this world.

Conversely, the use of this power by the good Precogs, and by those of us who eventually learn to be good Precogs, brings us closer to the paradise worlds, as we have paid the price.

I believe this is the true meaning of the "narrow path" or "narrow way".

Afterword

"Life can only be understood backwards, but it must be lived forwards." – Soren Kierkegaard

While I would tend to agree with Soren's statement about understanding the meaning of life, I believe that there are those who somehow sent their soul backward in time, or are remembering the future. These are the true high level Precogs. I have sometimes contemplated what it would be like to suddenly wake up in the past as if the last few decades have been a precognitive dream. How would I behave?

Then I have the flashback from my youth, those days in elementary school or middle school, being so naive.

Perhaps, after reading this book you are beginning to grok, the real secret, the cheat code. Perhaps now you remember crossing paths with a real Precog, looking back in hindsight?

That student who never seemed to make any mistakes, and whenever they spoke their words were carefully measured better than any adult.

> *"Row, row, row your boat,*
> *Gently down the stream.*
> *Merrily, merrily, merrily, merrily,*
> *Life is but a dream."*

www.ingramcontent.com/pod-product-compliance
Lightning Source LLC
Chambersburg PA
CBHW071453070526
44578CB00001B/327